Buddy the Wayward Wolverine

Mary A Livingston
Amanda Shufelberger

ILLUSTRATED BY
Tim Livingston

Red Tail Publishing
Anderson, CA
USA

Wolverine Sighted in California

Since the 1920's there were no scientifically documented sightings of wolverines in California. There were many tales of people seeing wolverines, but none confirmed. Then in 2008, a wildlife biologist documented a lone wolverine in the state. DNA sampling determined the 2008 wolverine was not from the California wolverines of the 1920's. His family was from Idaho.

Nobody knows how the wolverine, known as Buddy, came to be in California. This is an imagined story of how Buddy made his journey.

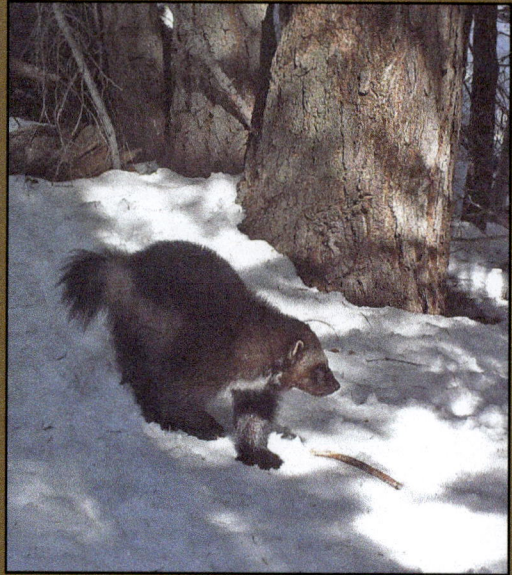

"Buddy" as captured by a carnivore study camera located on private timberland in the Sierras.
Photo courtesy Amanda Shufelberger

Red Tail Publishing
Established 1993

P.O. Box 1477, Anderson, CA 96007
www.redtail.com

Buddy, the Wayward Wolverine
ISBN 13: 978-0-9847756-5-1
Hardback Edition

Story ©2013 Mary A. Livingston & Amanda Shufelberger
Illustrations ©2013 Timothy J. Livingston
Critter Chit-Chatter™ © 2012 Red Tail Publishing,
Educational contributions by Amanda Shufelberger.
Critter Chit-Chatter™ and Working With Nature™ are trademarks of Red Tail Publishing.

f find us on Facebook

facebook.com/TheWaywardWolverine

facebook.com/RedTailPublishing

Buddy began his life in a snow den, deep in the Sawtooth Mountain Range of Idaho.

Wolverine kits are always hungry and compete for food. This is the way it is in the wild.

Mother wolverine taught her growing kits to hunt and scavenge for food. She also taught them about the dangers of people.

As Buddy got older, he ranged farther and farther from his family while looking for food. One day, Buddy smelled something new, something yummy.

Sniff, Sniff, Mmmm.

Buddy ignored his mom's warning about people. The tasty smell was too tempting. He reached out with his tongue for a lick.

TRAPPED!

Buddy could not free himself from the cage. He felt movement and heard strange humming sounds. A truck drove away with Buddy in the back.

When the truck stopped, Buddy smelled people. He growled. He did not like this, not one bit. Buddy was frightened and mad.

The wire door opened just a little and Buddy shot out.

When he stopped running, he had no idea where he was. The air and forest smelled different, but he was still hungry.

Sniff. Sniff. Mmmm.

Buddy followed the scent. He was very careful in his hunt and scored a fine meal.

Grrrrrr. Grrrrrr. A hungry bear
charged in and stole Buddy's food.
GRRRRRR. Buddy growled back.

The bear swiped with its big paw. Buddy ran into the woods without his meal.

Now he was hungry and thirsty.

Sniff. Sniff. Mmmm.

Following his nose, he found a drink in a water bucket. It seemed like a good place to hide. Buddy settled in for a nap at the fire station.

Whump-whump-whump.
Buddy awoke with a start.
Swoosh. He swung way
high into the air.
Whump-whump-whump.

The helicopter lowered the bucket to scoop water from the river.

Down, down, down, **kasplash!**

Swoosh! The rushing water swept Buddy out of the bucket. He climbed on a floating log to rest.

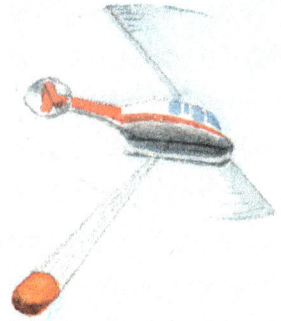

The river flowed faster and faster.
Buddy held on tighter and tighter.

Soon the water slowed.

Sniff. Sniff. Mmmm.

Buddy jumped up
over the rocks
to follow the scent
of yummy fish.
He snatched one.

To his surprise, the entire stringer of fish came along. He was so hungry he ate them all.

The next morning he heard people sounds.
He ran the other way.

Sniff. Sniff. Mmmm.

Buddy found food in a people camp. He gobbled it all down to the last crumb.

Again, he heard people. He hid in a dark place. While he was waiting for it to be safe, he took a nap.

Buddy awoke to a low humming sound and movement. He looked out another door from his hiding place.

Sniff. Sniff. Mmmm. Crunch. Crunch. Mmmm.

He didn't notice the RV coming to a stop.

Rrewrr. Rrewrrrrrrr.

Buddy couldn't see where the yowling was coming
from. He ducked back in the cabinet and darted out the
other side.

Buddy headed into the high country. His tummy grumbled.

Sniff. Sniff. Mmmm.

He found a deer carcass hidden under some trees. He pulled it out with his strong jaws and started his feast.

Grrrr. GRRRRR.

The owners of the meal returned and were not happy. The wolves circled. Buddy bit first. Yipe!

More wolves came. There were too many for Buddy to keep the meal. He had to fight to get away.

Buddy was very tired and still hungry. He stayed to himself as he wandered along.

Sniff. Sniff. Mmmm.

Food. **Sniff. Sniff.** Food and people. He was so hungry he followed the scent anyway.

He found an easy, yummy
meal left behind in a railcar.
Then he settled in for a nap.

Click. Clack. Clackity click.

Rumble. Rumble.

Buddy was moving so fast that he was afraid to open his eyes. Gathering his courage, he peered out.

Zooom. Russsssshhhhh.

Buddy ducked his head back in the boxcar and stayed very still.

Welcome to California

When the ruckus
stopped, Buddy jumped
clear of the train. He
decided to go where a
wolverine belonged. He
journeyed high into the
mountains, above where
the trees grow.

Buddy made the
Sierras of California
his new home.

Critter Chit-Chatter™

Wolverine

Name
The scientific name *Gulo gulo*, means "glutton glutton," because the wolverine will eat most anything. It is nicknamed *devil bear* and *skunk bear*. It is the largest land-dwelling member of Mustelidae (weasel) family.

Appearance
The wolverine has a dark brown pelage (fur) with a yellowish horizontal band around the body and a bushy tail. It resembles a small bear more than a weasel. It is not related to bears or wolves.

They have long, non-retractable claws.

Weight: 16 - 40 lbs.

Males are larger than females.

Habitat
Wolverine habitat is high boreal forests, usually above the treeline in the summer. It may inhabit lower elevations in the winter depending on food supply.

Males have larger home ranges with multiple females having territories within the range of the male. Home ranges are between 38-350 square miles.

Food
The wolverine eats mainly carrion (dead animals), but will consume a variety of foods depending on availability. It is an opportunistic feeder with a great sense of smell.

Reproduction
Litter size can range 1-5 kits. The average litter size is 2-3 kits.

Kits are typically born in deep snow dens dug by their mother.

Only mothers raise the young.

Behavior
The wolverine has a fierce reputation for challenging other predators over food.
It does not hibernate in winter, but usually goes lower in elevation to follow its food sources.

Wolverines are solitary animals except for the breeding season.

The Wolverine travels long distances over rough terrain and deep snow.

They may travel 30 to 40 miles a day searching for food. A young male searching for a mate may travel even farther.

Videos of the real Buddy.

You Tube Channel - SierraPacVideo - http://www.youtube.com/user/sierrapacvideo

"Buddy" - The Lone CA Wolverine http://goo.gl/ARLKQ

Buddy the Wolverine spottings in Sierra County, CA http://goo.gl/FHbwb

Watch this channel for new Buddy videos and more about people Working With Nature™.

To download Critter Chit-Chatter™ study guides go to www.redtail.com/workingwithnature

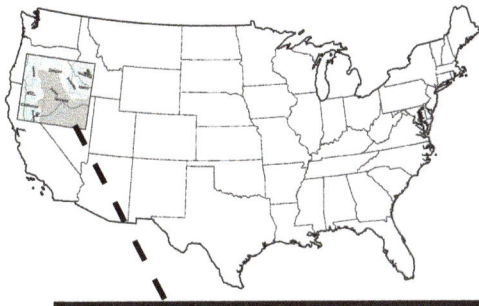

Buddy's Journey

Experts know from Buddy's DNA that his family is from the Sawtooth Range in Idaho. Buddy's fur samples also reveal isotopes that indicate he drank water from the same area in Idaho.

Wolverines are high mountain dwellers. There's no direct mountainous path from the Sawtooth Range of Idaho to the Sierra Nevada Range of California. Wolverines are elusive and avoid humans. It's possible that Buddy set out to establish his adult territory or find a mate. Some people speculate that a person may have illegally trapped and relocated Buddy to California.

How do you think Buddy travelled to California? It's fun to imagine Buddy's journey. No one knows the real story, except Buddy, and he isn't talking.

For more of Buddy's adventures in California, we hope you enjoy
Buddy and the Magic Chicken Tree.

www.ingramcontent.com/pod-product-compliance
Lightning Source LLC
Chambersburg PA
CBHW040257100426
42811CB00011B/1292